SOFT HUNGER

Also by r.h. Sin

Whiskey Words & a Shovel

Whiskey Words & a Shovel II

Whiskey Words & a Shovel III

Rest in the Mourning

A Beautiful Composition of Broken

Algedonic

Planting Gardens in Graves

Planting Gardens in Graves Volume Two

Planting Gardens in Graves Volume Three

She Felt Like Feeling Nothing

Empty Bottles Full of Stories

She Just Wants to Forget

Falling Toward the Moon

We Hope This Reaches You in Time

A Crowded Loneliness

She's Strong, but She's Tired

She Fits Inside These Words

Winter Roses after Fall

Dream, My Child

Anywho, I Love You

I Hope She Finds This

I Hope This Reaches Her in Time Revised Edition

Come Back to Me

This Day Is Dark

Beautiful Sad Eyes, Weary Waiting for Love

Ascending Assertion

A Midnight Moon

Read This If You've Been Ghosted

The Year of Letting Go

New Moons

My Dear Wildflower

Serenity's Song

The Quiet After

She Outgrew the Wound

SOFT HUNGER

the yearning

r.h. Sin

Andrews McMeel
PUBLISHING®

The authorised representative in the EEA is
Simon and Schuster Netherlands BV,
Herculesplein 96 3584 AA Utrecht, Netherlands.
(info@simonandschuster.nl)

Andrews McMeel Publishing
a division of Andrews McMeel Universal
1130 Walnut Street, Kansas City, Missouri 64106
www.andrewsmcmeel.com

26 27 28 29 30 RLP 10 9 8 7 6 5 4 3 2 1

ISBN: 979-8-8816-1204-7

Library of Congress Control Number: 2026935589

Editor: Danys Mares
Art Director: Diane Marsh
Production Editor: Elizabeth A. Garcia
Production Manager: Shona Burns

FSC
www.fsc.org
MIX
Paper | Supporting responsible forestry
FSC® C102842

I desire the kind
of closeness that grows
in the quiet
the kind that does not
ask for proof
I want the kind of love
that learns my silence
and answers softly

My soul felt you
before we met
the way a shore
knows the tide
There was a pull
long before
there was a touch

On those lonely nights
I keep your name
where prayer lives
When I breathe slowly
it rises, then settles
and the whole room
feels like a promise
rooted in all that you are

I would never rush the bloom
I water the soil
with patience
and witness the green
show its soft face

Some loves are storms
Ours begins quiet and calm
a change in the air
a pressure drop
a sky learning
a language of desire

I deserve the conversation
that happens without words
the one where eyes
carry a thousand small confessions

Your absence is a room
with a window
open to the sea
Everything I do
moves in and out
of that salt air

I practice wanting you like meditation
Inhale the touch of your hands
exhale the need to hurry

You teach me
that there is a softness
that is stronger than any heat
It stays; it steadies
It keeps the door unlocked
and the light on

I write letters
I never send
I fold them
into the shape of patience
I place each one
on the shelf of becoming

You are a slow light
on the horizon—
I learned to love
the distance
because it taught me
how to see you

I don't need fireworks
I want the ember
that refuses to die
the warmth that learns
my name and stays

I hunger for the part of you
that does not perform
Bring me the quiet
the weary, the honest
the unguarded
I will meet you there

If I could touch anything
I would touch the day
before it touches you
I would set down your burdens
beside the bed
and leave you only softness

I have learned that a heart
does not starve when it waits
It becomes precise
It chooses what feeds it

There is holiness in a hand
that does not rush
In that pause
the body hears
the truth
both of us
already know

I'm not asking for forever
I am asking for the kind of now
that feels like shelter after rain

You are the page
my pulse writes on
Every heartbeat leaves a small
warm sentence in the dark

I carry you the way
a secret carries heat
not to hide you
but to keep you alive
until the moment
says *yes*

I want to learn the shapes of your quiet joy
the smile no one sees
the relief when the world
finally lets you put your armor down

the pull

There is a devoted gravity
between us that language
will never be able to carry
Every word collapses
under the weight of us

If I could tell you
what this feels like
I would whisper
"A door opening
somewhere in my chest
a release of energy from the heart"

Every time I meet
your gaze
I lose another boundary

What a treat it would be
to get so lost in your grip
that the darkest parts of me
begin to blush and throb

I don't chase
I move slowly
like water finding
its level
and somehow I still
end up at your feet

There are people
who burn loud
and vanish
You burn quietly
and everything around you
begins to glow

You look at me
like you've already
imagined
how I taste
when I tell the truth

There are nights when I feel you
thinking of me
The air folds differently
My skin answers before
my mind does

You look at me
like you already know
the ending
and still want
to read it slowly

There's an ache in my chest
that doesn't hurt anymore
It sings

I imagine a shared meal
Me, at the table of essence
wet at the mouth
meeting your eyes
on the brink of ecstasy

When you speak
something ancient stirs
inside me
Something remembers
being wanted without fear

Somewhere between
your glance
and my restraint
we started a fire
that no one can see

I want to know
the shape of your silence
what it hides
what it heals

The pull between us
is not just desire
it's recognition

You touch me
in ways
that do not
require touch
You come in a way
that resembles art
a climax
worthy of museums

I don't need
to be understood
completely
I just need
to be held
correctly

the first time
our eyes met
it felt like the universe
exhaled and whispered
finally

In the back of my mind
I thought to myself
that if peace was the destination
she could ride me all the way to
tranquility

the bloom

You opened me
with patience
no force
no noise
only the kind of quiet
that makes flowers
brave enough to bloom

Every time you speak
the room changes shape
my guard dissolves
and I become light

There is a tenderness in you
that reminds me of early morning
calm but capable of everything

You didn't rush my healing
you waited until I was ready
to feel safe again

I love the way you see through me
not to expose but to understand

This is what it feels like
when softness wins

I am learning that love
can be both still and wild

Your hands have a way of saying
You are safe here
without using a single word

Every moment with you
teaches me that affection
doesn't have to be earned

You listen like

it's an act of devotion

I want to grow
inside your quiet

You became my favorite
form of peace

There are no fireworks
between us
only a steady flame
that refuses to go out

Daydreaming
about the nights
when your spine reaches
for the sky
like the moon rising up
to kiss midnight

The way you look at me
makes time slow down
until it remembers
what forever feels like

I stopped needing grand gestures
when I realized
how powerful presence could be

You make me want to become
someone gentler
someone who believes
in love again

There's beauty in being loved slowly
It's a softness that doesn't ask
only offers

You love me in a language
that doesn't hurt

Healing once felt impossible
until you showed me
that love could be quiet too

the confession

I have loved before
but not like this
not with my whole silence

I could spend a lifetime
counting the inches
of my own existence
vanishing inside of you

The truth is
I was afraid to be known
You made it feel safe

Sometimes I look at you and think
So this is what peace looks like
when it wears a human face

I spent years
convincing myself
I didn't need anyone
You arrived
and reminded me
that needing can be gentle
soft and easy

You seem to ask
the kind of questions
that feel like permission
a need for entry
a desire to go deeper

I didn't just fall for you
I remembered what love
was always meant
to feel like
because of you

Missing you
means remembering
the version of me
that can only be seen
with your eyes
and felt at the tips
of your fingers

You saw through every
defense I built
and stayed
where so many
have left

I used to hide my softness
because the world called it weak
You call it art

You make me believe
in the kind of love
that doesn't demand
performance

Every word I've written
before this
was practice for your name
rehearsal for your presence

I am not afraid of losing you
I am afraid of forgetting
what it feels like to be known
and recognized by your eyes
your soul and hands

Loving you has felt like
praying for an impossible thing
made tangible by your existence

You remind me
that truth doesn't always
need to hurt to heal

You are the person
who didn't try to fix me
and that is when
my heart started to change

Sometimes love
doesn't save us
it reveals us

I never want to own you
I want to honor you

The moment I stopped
pretending to be strong
I found the kind
of strength that lasts

the waiting

I have learned that absence
is not always loss
Sometimes it's the universe
giving love time to grow roots

You are everywhere
and nowhere
a heartbreak echoing
through the spaces
I once called lonely

Even in your silence
I feel seen
covered and protected

I do not chase
I become still enough
for what is meant for me
to find me

This waiting is not empty
It's filled with the small miracles
that come from becoming
and unfolding into love

You taught me that timing
is also an act of love

I hold the memory of your voice
like sunlight
in a closed hand

I have made a home
in the space between
now and when

Sometimes the heart knows
before the world does

This distance isn't cruel
it's clarifying

I no longer fear solitude
I've met too many parts
of myself there

If it's real
it will find me
I don't have to demand it

You are the ache
that makes me patient

The world tells us to hurry
but love unfolds
in its own time

Somehow I knew
that waiting for you
would bring me home
to every part of me
that I believed was lost

Your name lingers
between my lips
a quiet echo I can't release
a hunger I can't silence

the becoming

I ache for the way
your hands trace poetry
along my nervous system
pulling confessions
from my body
without a single word

I am undone by the thought of you—
the curve of your spine
the electricity in your palms
the heat of your breath
the truth hidden in your sigh

Your absence cuts deeper
than teeth
sharper than a razor's edge

Midnight without you is hollow
Even the sheets grow cold
without the weight of your body
without the warmth of your desire

There's a stairway
to heaven
in the way
you arch your back
a place for me to rise

Soft and immense hunger
is the memory of your shoulder
and the softness of your lips
haunting me at dawn
when the bed is wide
and unforgiving

My love, soft hunger is not starvation
it is the ache between breaths
the pause before
a wild and deep surrender

She taught me that love can be a gentle bite
teeth, at times like velvet
pressed into the spaces no one else
can touch

The night continues in
wild surrender.